Praise for Carmen Firan's Poetry

Carmen Firan's poetic voice rings with qualities that are familiar to American poets. Beyond the tumult of politics and the drama of the past decade—though these have their say—the poetry of this generation is joined by strong linguistic and musical concerns. Since moving to New York, Firan has been writing poems that explore the new world. Her dual perspective enables her to offer fresh insights about the United States and about Romania, each mirroring some aspects that are poetically surprising. This book of poems brings an exciting view of life, love, and the meaning of existence, through the eyes of a renowned East European poet.

—*Andrei Codrescu*

Carmen Firan's beautiful and powerful poems, charged with gloom and passion, recreate her struggles not only with life and love, with her history and ours (and "its bloody hangover of the senses"), but with the beasts of language, whether invasive or voracious or fugitive. In this war of words, armed with her "dialect of Old Angelic," she indisputably wins.

—*Harry Mathews*

Who is Carmen Firan? A voice broken by exile like glass shattered against a rock. But all these pretty shards, in the naked light, said something, too, to this woman who can't leave language alone; and patiently she gathered them, risking the cuts, to fashion a new, fractured voice for a New World because she was tired of being an old self trapped in an old country "who stands waiting on a train platform like a tree grown in the cracks of the asphalt"; and although she came to find new cities but found instead a sinking city like New Orleans, in which "shutters from colonial houses float downriver" and "coffins wrapped in Mardi Gras beads carry the last pharaohs of the food-can pyramids," and saw herself "running voiceless through concentric waves," she kept speaking and kept writing, even if it were just to describe the fact that "death swims on her back" and thus brought us the gift of her wonderful words that became the swirling pages of this wonderful book.

—*Bruce Benderson*

Carmen Firan writes with knife-edge precision of our apocalyptic world. Firan would believe herself "invented to be masterless" but, like us all, is haunted by "yesterday's household snake." It is a world, at times, of deceptive calm where "death swims on her back." It is a world of betrayals and deceit: it is, therefore, our world but rarely understood and rendered with such crisp clarity.

—*Edward Foster*

Carmen Firan's subtle yet vividly intense writings of the artist's inner life range from Bucharest and New York to invented submarine and subterranean landscapes of mind. Mixed in with her bitter memory of an oppressive totalitarian society is her sparkling ironic wit.

—*Isaiah Sheffer*

Rock and Dew

– Selected Poems –

Carmen Firan

The Sheep Meadow Press
Riverdale-on-Hudson, New York

Designed and typeset by The Sheep Meadow Press
Distributed by The University Press of New England

All inquiries and permission requests should be addressed to the publisher:

The Sheep Meadow Press
PO Box 1345
Riverdale, NY 10471

Library of Congress Cataloging-in-Publication Data is available upon request.

ISBN: 978-1-931357-63-0

ALSO BY CARMEN FIRAN:

<u>Poetry</u>

Inhabited Words, 2007
Disconsolate Conquests, 2004
In The Most Beautiful Life, 2002
The First Moment after Death, 2001
Accomplished Error, 2000
Punished Candors, 2000
Places for Living Lonely, 1999
Pure Black, 1995
Staircase under the Sea, 1994
Tamer of Stolen Lives, 1984
Paradise for Monday, 1983
Illusions on My Own, 1981

<u>Fiction</u>

Words & Flesh, 2008
The Second Life, 2005
The Farce, 2003
Getting Closer, 2000

<u>Screenplay</u>

Stars' Owner
Dream Trap
A Trio for Inferno
Light in the Attic

Acknowledgments

Grateful acknowledgment to the editors and publishers of the following journals where poems in this book first appeared: *Arshile, Asheville Poetry Review, Ars Interpres, Barrow Street, The Broome Review, Breathe, Connotation Press, Exquisite Corpse, Free Verse, Hanging Loose, Hubbub, Interpoezia, Literary Chaos, The Light Millennium, Notre Dame Review, Osiris, Ozone Park Literary Journal, Paper Street, The Poetry Miscellany, Salt River Review, Talisman, Words Without Borders, Yellow Medicine Review,* and the anthology, *Twenty Years After the Fall,* (Decatur: Wising Up Press) and in anthologies of poetry in USA, Ireland, UK, Israel, France, Germany, Italy, Poland & Romania.

Many thanks to my translators Adam J. Sorkin, Andrei Codrescu, Isaiah Sheffer, and Julian Semilian, and also to Nina Cassian, Maurice Edwards and Alexandra Carides for their permanent support of my poetry. Adam J. Sorkin expresses gratitude to the University College of Penn State University and the Penn State Brandywine campus for support of his work on the translations in this volume.

All my gratitude goes to Stanley Moss for his inspiring work in editing the English versions of the poems and for making possible the publication of this book.

CONTENTS

I *INHABITED WORDS*

II *MY SLEEP IS NOT MY OWN*

I

INHABITED WORDS

Translations by Adam J. Sorkin & the poet

stars and crosses

1.

I was born at a crossroads
on a night with stars and crosses

no word was in place

the conquerors were licking their wounds
already contriving further utopias
parents kept throwing stones against the house
while history turned the other cheek
and hurried to wash its sins as new wolves
primped their hair before parallel mirrors

the fates showed up late
benevolent and lazy
they hardly glanced at me as I arranged words
on a knife blade
they didn't even flinch when the first drop of blood
stained the Iranian rug looted by a sailor
from countries impossible to reach

2.

to this day the scar on my index finger
is proof that this all really happened
when uninvented animals congregated in the back garden
and fixed me with phosphorescent eyes
forcing me to admit their being
and bring them inside
where everybody waited for this circus to end
and dinner to begin

I saw them: beasts with human voices
figments of words among which I fumbled
aiming not to displease
just as later I'd write poems
only after my lovers had gone to sleep

I was born after the flood and before the thaw
neither night nor day
at an intersection of empires which led nowhere
exactly there the fields gnaw stone
and every raindrop is a conspiracy against the desert
during the day you muffle sobs in your fists
at night you steal a bearskin from the forest
the heroes of my land don't have necks
they hide golden eggs so deep in the sand
not even they can find them again

3.

in the central station where you catch the express
for the army or the capital
I waited patiently for yellow submarines
the years flew by with illusions blowing
like the flowers on my mother's summer dress

then to satisfy the fates
—they're still laughing their heads off—
I moved into a snail with windows facing south
and a perfect view: the cemetery on the hill
the ocean at my feet
a new century of stars and crosses

the soul poured into bottles floats wherever it will

the shirt of water

I inhabit a word
I moved in with my weapons, possessions and sins
ignoring my parents' advice:
don't build a house with a staircase to heaven
don't lie to yourself
when loneliness forsakes you for a brief fling
don't yearn for anyone else's illusions
and never never fall in love
with your own word, the sinful soul

this space is narrow
we can feel each other's breath—
air-vowels, earth-consonants
I pay my bills when due
and turn off the lights after every syllable
I'd consider myself a lucky tenant
except that night after night my dreams grow louder
and force me to face the unspoken
which can no longer be shut away in my extravagant shelter

then my own word occupies me like a ghost
he slips his treacherous tongue inside my unwritten pages
though enslaved, he wants me to obey only him
as my master—
the lead tips of whips crack at the world's end

I live in a word as in a shirt of water
at its seams I feign freedom
chewed-up metaphors glued to my eyelids
my master tastes his own weakness
on the tip of his tongue

soon

soon
I'll grow old

you won't hear me
snow will cover my traces
one morning I'll wake up beside you
and open the curtain
convinced that through the window
I can see the Himalayas from above
a cynical miracle achieved without the least effort
lion cubs will spring forth ravenous
tear out my heart bolting it down

you don't believe in the devouring word
until sound and soul join each other
you'll hear only the crunch of the poem
in their young jaws

eclipse

everything passes, you told me,
as when on a high-speed train you look out the window
and the trees rush behind you
with the mist of each word on a winter morning

everything passes, you said,
with the thick soup dribbling from grandma's chin
to the edge of a hospital bed
with a pressed violet in an encyclopedia
whose pages no one will ever turn

everything passes,
the waters grows calm
the blare of sounds will blur—
the shadow sets upon the body

differences

the difference between solemnity and a rigid pair of shoulders
is the same as between pretended silence and speechlessness
the parallel lines race each other leaving no trace on the skin
they flow between heaven and earth
linking big infinity with small infinity

the difference between loneliness and a languorous woman
recumbent on a divan
is the same as between imposed exile and running in circles
far enough from home

with your fate recast halfway through your journey
in the midst of others' silence
you could die and no one would hear

real estate

I have a house for sale in a quiet neighborhood
only a couple of steps from hell
—location is everything—
the dead body always exits feet first
and is tempted to run downhill
while the soul gets yanked free through a window
by a well-intentioned grandmother
who sacrificed her day
to show off the banquet high in the heavens

I have a house for sale with new roof and triple-glazed windows,
it comes down to predicting the future
the dead will want perfect isolation
high ceilings to keep cool in the summer
and to give the impression of open space,
the sky a stone's throw away,
the city the third stop on the express line,
the best yeshiva just around the corner

for quite a while now
I've tried to sell the house roof walls and me,
the timing's bad, my Chinese neighbors suggest
suspicious of the grapevine
which throws black grapes over their fence
mimicking my childhood transplanted into a foreign body,
people are no longer in a rush to buy,
the planet keeps getting warmer,
everything's growing, enlarging, swelling
we'll pop like a balloon,
spread throughout the universe
and create other utopias

OK, but in the here and now
I have an old brick house for sale
motionless on the threshold I'm waiting for
buyers from other planets—
please hurry, it's not even my house

reincarnation

neither young nor pretty
I flit about in a cheap summer dress
with the body of a dead bird
I synchronize my heartbeats
to the flutter of wings before the sudden fall
to the time elapsed since a finger squeezed the trigger
until the first lost feather floated
over the ocean

I recognize the scrap of sky in my mother's belly
her blue scarf
wraps around my neck
it severs

crackups

in my late thirties I killed my ego
in the bathroom
I slowly twisted its neck with my own two hands
the Adam's apple thudded to the cement floor
one by one I cut the threads
from which I drew my power
strong enough to keep me upright in a hunchback world

I knew I was mistaken to love my crackups
more than the patch of earth granted to me
now I know that each departure
is nothing more than the self-importance
of not being the one who stands
waiting on the platform
a tree grown in the cracks of the asphalt

in cold blood I watched the warm, proud, salty stream
snake down its chin
washing away the arrogance of forgiving nothing
the sweet venom of my daily solitude with an impudent body
the bread and butter of my youth

counter-season

winter is yours
the city empty and quiet as if evacuated
it gets dark early and stays dark
you approach me quietly
and at each step something disappears irrevocably
swallowed by the earth's hunger for mystery

summer is mine
only the echo of packed-down snow reaches
the tremor of your voice in an open field
white as a bed sheet

I press my palms over my eyes
in the end darkness looks the same:
the tunnel that spits you out and the one that sucks you back
I draw the curtains over a counter-season
from which no one has ever returned

letter from the world's metropolis

you'd think we're not so alone
among so many secondhand champions

an exiled poet left the faucet on
out of toxic words grow flowers
whose color has swallowed their perfume
gardens of plastic and cardboard
patriotic melancholy supersized
for prizes bought on a summer vacation

we're told to drink plenty of water
the empire is whitening its teeth rejuvenating
and labors tirelessly for those ambushed
by immortality and depression
well behaved, we are mute and blind
astonished not to find in our guide to manners
the Romanian word *dor* we much long for
at MoMA the DaDa exhibition flatters our history
friday evenings admission is free
and so are we
vibrating like slow bells for the fallen
as a new day for the world began
in Burma, China, Karakorum—
burned out the hollow where the night was frozen
the roll call ended, and the brief flame;
and still we lingered by the tomb
long after the sun had risen.

requiem for the sinking city

it takes naiveté to believe the tales
of the old knife thrower
the blues dancer on the alligator's back
from which he'll fashion evening bags
and binding for books
written in the language of dream
madmen who with sound and fury besiege
the streets of the Vieux Carré

shutters from colonial houses float downriver
coffins wrapped in Mardi Gras beads
carry the last pharaohs of the food-can pyramids

the blind saxophonist sets his shoes to dry in a voodoo-shop window
he snaps his soul down as if dealing
the fool from whom the archangel tattooed with blue hearts
bets against crew-cut angels
witches fly on a single wing aborting babies
little clay devils who cavort among dancers' feet

it takes naiveté to believe that this century will ever wake up
from its bloody hangover of the senses
the world's placenta bubbles muddy waters

death swims on her back
pulling behind her the last streetcar

a peaceful afternoon

the sky congealed in a cup
yolk spilling over the rim—
sunset above the hospital

in the windows white gowns wave
a surrender to night
tomorrow some will be carried out on their shields

I lean on the casement sill and listen
the boats come home empty from the sea
the fishermen disembark

a natural death of a peaceful afternoon:
youth hurtles like an avalanche in the mountains
then drifts like a summer vacation

face to face

silence blackens the walls
with our attenuated shadows
two smoke-dancers

in the bedroom suspended high above the city
deafening noises pass by
with the threat of so many losses
with the ashes of so many futile victories

yesterday's household snake
coiled in a corner
watches cynically and waits

what we weren't given

write your poems by tomorrow
scrub the walls
wash the sea thoroughly
so nothing remains
no memories, not time or measure
no trace of joy or pain
you need the sense that you've cleaned,
tidied up, forgotten
you had a say and closed your eyes
then maybe the overlooked word
will lick your feet

obsessions

always the same dreams
the thump on hot bed sheets
after each flight
wing-traces well hidden
for fear of ridicule
next morning
when light screams into your life
canceling every rule
distance and time claim their rights

I go running voiceless through concentric waves
submerged in dead seas
swallowed alive by quicksand
pursued by bodies with blank faces
I can't manage to close the door to the beyond
in delirium I save my breath
abandoned to destiny's hands
that can restart a drowned man's heart
long after the soul has entered another shell

nothing is more shameful than dream shame
alone surrounded by famished eyes and mouths
a grotesque ballet in the absence of words

conspiracy

as soon as I turn my gaze
flowers bloom
nuns throw off their habits and cowls
and raise their eyes to the sky as if everything's there
the river shrugs out of its channel
larvae dress in iridescent butterfly wings
so as to confound our expectations
neglected objects withdraw into themselves
and conspire against separation—
time-worn ropes tethered to a pair of fixed points:
the water we emerged from and the water we pass into
floating white petals blush
as soon as I turn my gaze

chaos

every night I choose a word
and repeat it endlessly until it loses its meaning

the syllables tangle together
in a language uninvented
mysterious and cold, rough and absurd
abandoned a long time ago

the vowels lose their luster
scalded like mollusks thrown in boiling water
while the stubborn consonants try to keep the rhythm

the word becomes a clod of clay
I keep repeating it like a transgressor of language
who cannot control such sinful joy

the sounds come unglued one by one
petals plump with blood and nails
stellar debris floats in the air
and sticks at random to ceiling and floor
to a chair or my clothes,
my dress fills with fragments of words,
short vowels with a twisted neck, stubby syllables,
pompous letters, mountain peaks and clumps of algae,
square verses or angelic corners, diaphanous stencils
on the edge between revelation and madness

I continue to repeat the same word
until it's flayed of its flesh
a phalange pointing at heaven taking it to task
until the darkness of the beginning
when all that's left is deafening tumult

halves

everything I try to tell you stops halfway
I utter the first sound but the word has no patience
it rolls its consonants rapidly—
a fish bone stuck in the throat
far enough back not to know
whether the air is whistling out
or wheezing in

neither my exhaustion nor my fear
will ever reach you
I'm a rocket launcher with an empty barrel
a juggler whose hat has been stolen

roused from sleep in the middle of the night
death rolls over
bare soles sticking out from under the thin sheets

uncoupling

angels are neither bird
nor mankind
it's useless for us to represent
their chubby child-like body
with pelican wings
over a bed
or in a bitter corner of the temple

coupled words
are angels
born from the illusion of another life
impossibly perfect

the year of the dog

I search for a trace of myself in the bed of leaves
under a stone warmed by a swarm of souls
that make room for me
I take aim at the star I fell from once upon a time
maybe on purpose, maybe by mistake—
half centaur, more than half human

my passing here is no more than a rehearsal
for the long journey on the wooden dog's back
I synchronize my breath to his
the power hidden in affected weakness
the terror of foreseeing the end of the road
when like dandelions brightening a field bathed by moonlight
the beloved dead will lead me by the hand

I measure the earth with my palm
clenched around the heart

heirlooms

our objects will survive us
with pride in their own faith
liberated from the soul
we lent them
ready to obey
a new master
just as on the morning after death
the light will fall the very same way
on the red-poppy quilt
your aunt's gift
to calm our fear—
the new tenant will use it
to wrap his hunting rifle

pageants

full of the aberration of victory
helmets and bright trumpets glorifying the fear
of remaining the sole conquerors of the Earth

women with plastic breasts
sway their hips in the lambada after each battle cry

veterans suck oxygen from a tube
with the fumes of past empires

the rows of chairs in the sun remain empty

acrobats keep to their steady diet of tumbling

the Pope proffers love with a gospel rhythm
prepared for resurrection in his pointy red slippers

the parade on the main boulevard
can be watched from all the corners of the world
electronic screens in Times Square mix the digits:
today's temperatures, the body count of the drowned,
babies born in India,
the percentage of the obese
who will guzzle the last drop of the Persian Gulf

cuckolded men, expectations dashed,
exiles' dreams hung out to dry,
the irony of destiny and a cacophony of laughter
after each experiment,
petals rain from the sky
inside-out manifestos
urging peace and order
dancers resigned to wooden legs

we flee from ourselves

ad the cliffs are golden sandstone

absence

the gleaming wood floor trembles
like a tree felled young
the heart constricts into a bitter kernel
your pearl necklace hangs cockeyed on a closet door
inside, my best years are stored
their days tangled

your whispers rustle at the bottom of a closed drawer
among quince flowers with a mothball scent
and faded photographs with frayed corners—
time stopped for no good reason
except to bring sight to its knees

game

death has withdrawn in a corner
curled up in a ball
tired of sucking and gnawing
yet she's just an old crone
gently she rebukes me:
—dearie, would you like me to go away?
so I invite her to stay

I try trading the bird's neck for my own
this way it will be much easier
I know her gnarled hands must cause her pain

the old woman cackles with glee
thinking I was scheming to fly
not die
—put back your stony neck, please
don't you see I'm just trying to tease?

the place where no one dies

all the words we have spoken
gather in one place

the walking sticks of wanderers through earth's entrails
abandoned following the fatal leap from the heights
lean against one another
ruined mountains of air and wood

ahead of us and behind, silence as at the beginning
molecules sputtering in a fiery crater
sounds transformed by the solar plexus
conjugated according to new rules
embodying us

comedown

fall comes with a bent back
no matter what I'm under its hump
emptiness jabs its poison needle in my neck
I wake up cornered by cold
much older than my hands
than my mother—
unheard I shriek a poem of mud
time aims a grass bullet at me
my shoulders hump over one by one

the tyranny of the word

he ties my hands to the table leg
turns on the TV
cleans the glass from which I drink my daily dram
of ashes topped with a drop of light
and forces me to listen to him to his final letter
until metal bars bloom in my transparent flesh

everybody demands the truth—
the empty word whines in my ear
gulping down metaphors rind and pits—
and I have only my toothless mouth
how high can I raise my cry
for how long my song

I was invented to be masterless
I devour things by chance
and let myself be devoured with moderation,
naked and quiet I sound—the empty word tells me—
then I break my chains and flee with the first syllable

delirium

I woke up with a dry mouth
in my dream I'd told you everything that could be said

rain kept falling upward and the water dissolved
my enemies' names with shoe polish labels
floating together, sodden and swollen,
on a street where once I strolled
for the sole pleasure of the conspiring in dreams
with such loneliness my men stretched out their necks
and flew in fluttering capes
like bats scattered over the city

I was the only inhabitant
of a blue cup
terribly thirsty
but there's never been a thirst truly quenched

suppositions

what would the savior have looked like
grown old
would he still have lent
his severe, nostalgic face
to the builders of churches
to the arrogant destroyers in quest of myths
or guilty would he have healed
his own joints
letting the water remain water
while the blind fumbled along their way

would he have given his last son
to doubt
or in the evening
laying his head on Magdalene's knees
would he have seen the earth as round
spinning on her index finger

the banquet

at the great banquet
we're served *ahs*
in Chinese porcelain and Bohemian crystal
everywhere a festive clink, an air of celebration

on the tip of our tongues we try a morsel of treason
it tastes like rabbit stuffed into the ring around a dove's eye
on gigantic trays with dragons painted cardinal red
we're served fear in aspic
and the guests lean back in their chairs
with shivers of pleasure and panic

there arrive new kinds of speech, adoration and lamentation
in thinly sliced words time whines milky in the glasses
on the table cloth vanity drips from the candle holders
in orange syllables

there is an art in knowing how to combine the letters
so as to manage your ego, your weight, your rage
how to nourish your pride with purple accents
or to choose what to taste first
either humility on little plates
or creamed patience with the sharp tang of Roquefort

we gulp, we quaff, we guzzle down words
the feast drains our minds, stuffs our souls
in a far corner history drapes a full-dress cape
over her bare shoulders

leftovers

the dead arrange their white silhouettes in a circle
and whirl dizzily over our foreheads
the storm of things left unfinished
tosses dreams to the ground
sleep comes from an instinct for self-defense
from the fear of not being sucked in through air-mouths,
of not being seduced by their mute song
vibrating in our joints

the eye of the all-powerful
levels abysses and mountain peaks—
on a plate of dull colors
leftovers look the same

a terrible wind howls in the sky

rock and dew

to Nina

you sit on a lotus leaf and a bed of nails
every morning
you wash your memory with angel water
and swallow ground egos
dipped in wax tears

time raps at the window with a cloven hoof

in your blood flow men and words
losses and abandonment
small points of pride in a crazed mirror

the hourglass draws back its hot sand

with a slender arm you detach the world
from the earth's eye socket
there rushes forth a bird of rock and dew—
forever radiant
sublimely desperate

counterfeits

how many words do we need to make ourselves clear?

in cubicles and cells papered with thick letters
we throw each other all-purpose slogans
air balls that slam us in the chest, knock us down
flying erratically—
awkward counterfeits in the absence of genuine wings
used only in commercials for organic chickens
raised by fake farmers
somewhere between Earth and Mars

for how long can the orphic whispers distract death
from its course over bright cliffs
where trembling silhouettes are the only thing you can see?
how loudly can we wail smothered inside these four walls?
the most secret thought is as comfortable
on the therapist's couch as in a gas station
where they sell roses by the dozen,
the most private feeling flickers on computer screens,
no metaphor is listed on the stock market of words
camouflaged in barrels of solitude

on an old leather map
the rivers of childhood stay their course swollen with dreams

sorrow draws the masks from the face

last impression

nothing matters—
an aged courtesan confided to me
twirling a cigarette
between indigo lips
God's always somewhere else
bored by error and backbiting
merciless even to his own brood
he hides either in provocative words
or in etched faces
according to his inexplicable taste
for half-baked martyrs—
otherwise we wouldn't stick it out here
chewing our helplessness like honest camels
abandoned at the first sandstorm

darkness reaches us

after the matinee the last ballerinas have gone
beggars on the night shift
brokers with slack jaws
exhausted nurses gluing fish scales
over the dark circles under their eyes
mornings of *haute couture*
choked in gunpowder
in the succulent smell of hamburgers
grilled on the Great Wall
beyond which all you can see
is an endless expanse of sand with beached whales

darkness reaches us like a screen lowered
truth stifles its seeking
the mouths of sinners lined up against the wall
guilty of their own illusions
swallow their words
troubling the silence settled like a deliberate fog
on the clairvoyants' eyes

birds of prey circle above the city
the conquerors swallow their swords

false memories

a well-hidden thought is enough
for fear to grip you to the bone
the sleepwalker stalking through others' dreams
with white illusions and false memories—
tragedy deceived by loose reins
the imagination bought off with alternative destinies

alone with our own words
rolling like beads of ink
on glossy paper that absorbs nothing
no shelter at home they stand by the fence in line
or curl up in dusty corners with all sorts of pronouncements
other lives with doors wide open face the wall
this never-ending to-and-from—
diamonds in fine gravel
with the pretense of a moment's glitter—
perfect imitations

from above it looks just the same

if that autumn morning hadn't happened
the hot exhalations of the beheaded city
the silence fallen like a lead curtain
we still would have kept hedging our bets
on fancied battles
imaginary geographies

the strong are lonely
the strong are sad
vulnerable in the candor
of pressing their desire so far
they can no longer follow their tracks by eye

from above it looks just the same:
the dead with the dead
the living with the worthless

meeting

you arrived at dusk
the threshold of my house had run away
loneliness had stepped outside

I'm not afraid, I told you
look, my bloods grows tall as a tree
it breaks the ceiling, spurts high overhead
I don't rule the word
look, I'm ruled by the unspoken
and because you're here, too
watch the mountain enter the city
don't you feel its rocks crush us?

I feel nothing, you answered,
and taking my hands you ripped my heart out
threw it against the mountain
and I fly away

the caretaker of dreams

in every dream I speak a different language
and in every language words have a different color
blind dreams rise from their foreheads
inflated on the purple horizon

from all I said in my lives before and to come
there remain only the flight path, the wing's whisper
the island where I took refuge
free inside so many walls
on which I scratch neither hearts or love-words
but signs in the language I speak while asleep
a dialect of Old Angelic still useful for crossing borders

I have a vocation for happiness
a sort of unconscious facility
at making an ally of the caretaker of dreams
who's always ready to lend me the silk cocoon
in which words sneak past customs
intimate objects I carry with me undeclared

nothing's to be done about my golden dowry
dead languages yield just the powdery dust of stars

impromptu

I've always lived in imagination
which doesn't mean I could prevent
the collapse of my interior constructions
even this house with its cracked threshold
doesn't enter my fantasies

I can still pack my angel under my arm and take off
—the child, the fur coat, the photos
the poems written sunny afternoons in the kitchen—
and make believe I'll go home
to the empty house where the windows and doors
tremble all by themselves

faces

at the beginning only words came between us
paper boats that float just beyond
the horizon patched with my illusions
where eyes redden
and lines of equilibrium turn inside out
like a winter coat worn at the sleeves

in the beginning you thought me wise
you'd set your face beside mine in the mirror
then you covered my face with your hand

where colors still have sounds

I'm writing to tell you:
keep away from death

she'll come again anyway
wrapping her egg
in a nest of bright wires
run as far as you can
every evening around nine
when her finger weighs down
the hand of the alarm clock
another dead weight
this old man a bit to the right,
that woman even farther,
a row of birds on the window ledge
pecking at my heart

she guards your threshold
like a trusty watchdog
lest you lavish too much of yourself on this world
that needs no more than
your name on a sheet of paper

I snap her spine
and flee as far as I can
where colors still have sounds
blind—she helps me cross the street
she knows me by sight

on the other side
a silent black dog sits and waits

II

MY SLEEP IS NOT MY OWN

my sleep is not my own

o, lord, death fears me
he touches me lightly
then jumps away like a child
and trembles
his finger on my lips
not disingenuous as it might seem
gentle and whole he smiles at me

I take his hand and force him
to stroke and tender my sleep
as it lies stretched on a bed sheet

his hand draws back:
I can't—he whispers—
your slumber is too cold
and yet, and yet
something in you draws me,
and I could hold you
and I could tell you tales and tales,
your eye draws me,
I am inside its globe,
teach him silence
I fear its expression
and I can't hear or see myself

Translated by Andrei Codrescu

to the very last

the loved ones
and those not loved
depart one by one

the sand slips through our fingers
to the very last grain

even the heart of the poet
freezes up

let thy will be done
and give us not
so much death
in one single life

Translated by Julian Semilian

high subterranean galleries

poems displayed in the public square,
crucified dolls,
icons of rejected dreams

I look out the window at ice blocks
gliding on the lake like white coffins
sailing towards a world
without passion or blood

I look out the window at the city's hump,
at the city's wounds,
wet as the muzzle of a mad dog

I descend into the high
subterranean galleries,
plagued by a winter of humiliation

the old she-wolf, weeping,
has devoured her young

Translated by Isaiah Sheffer

the woman of sand

I would like to have been wise
to be spared having to discover
there are no sins
that our passage through life wasn't on purpose,
to believe in the destiny
of the melancholy conquerors
turning wine into blood or water
and to speak with reserve
frightened by all the old proverbs,
saws and warnings told by the wise
who never respected anything but genius
and preserved nothing except flawlessness
from which the cynics nurse their eternity
the way the ocean follows its sensuality
and always sips from the beach
some woman of sand

in the most beautiful life possible
I hold with my breast the noise
of the most beautiful metropolis
smiling enigmatically each time
I have to justify its madness
when I find myself sketched
the perfect trace
of its finger in the sand

Translated by Julian Semilian

the end in India

1.

there are neither disappearances nor separations
only meanderings of the mind
what remains after nothing remains
is the soul pulverized into air and walls,
the unbeing just as illusory as the flesh

2.

over there what began will never be ended
where the sun rises from the river on a shield
where Earth rotates with nowhere to go
under the dried-up hump of the fiery cow
over there the idols rest serene in the sun,
they share eternity in small cups of saffron
mixing up bodies and exchanging souls
at daytime playing death with ironic patience
only at sunset to start all over again

3.

the promise of death delayed
agonizing wrecks on the stairs to heaven
with its face of a famished saint

the fire is smoldering on the pyre
lit up by ageless men
the destroyer blows the ashes of a girl
on a bee's wing

from above only the smirk of ravens
the illusion of the ultimate death

4.

how much of us is by mere chance
and how much by intended errors
which breath can choose its body
when all one can see through a hole in the sky

are white and steady stairs
the ribs of god hauling its resignation through the desert
pilgrims sipping from the sacred hoof
the water of a foreign empire

5.

I no longer know what shame is
nor the humility of having thoughts
but also this body towards which God's finger
points out professionally my vulnerable spots

who could tell that poems are written with the same hand
that rummages on the shroud yellow flowers
some pieces of words left unlived
the destroyer is a riot of colors and dye
he sits his legs crossed and plays with a bone baton
over the bent heads,
he captures the flying soul of the dead
sucks out his atoms and blows them into our joints,
spherical forms of fog in search of vehicles
to carry the eternal transparency

6.

we will return over here unseen
on the wing of an insect
or in the skin of a snake
we will quietly unfold our sheets,
lotus will spring from our joints
with delicate necks
moving our world from above
so we can reach with our bare feet the sunset
neither sky nor earth
neither human nor bird
only life chopped-up on a tray
from which cynical gods
taste and spit in turn

Translated by Andrei Codrescu

blue poems

raindrops of ink
falling on the cold stones

up above
death cracks his whip

and in each blue poem
there is a story
wrenched out of the streets
like a nail ripped
from the belly of a ship

Translated by Isaiah Sheffer

it snowed—that's all

sometimes
He descends through my soul
in my chest I feel the earth's weight
under His heel
pressing on mine

in the lightened sky
a firm line
a sword will fall
under it my slender throat settles

one sudden morning
man was given the Word
that reigned alone

one sudden morning
you part the curtain
and see that it snowed
what more can you do,
what else can you do?!
it snowed——that's all

the curtain wraps itself
around your throat

Translated by Andrei Codrescu

in the absence of love

the sea sighs like woman
but in this sigh I only hear
the breath of a haunted man

yellow beach flowers,
wild stones,
salt drops which sting my arms
two salty seagulls
swoop out of my eyes
and fly side by side
crying out to one another
over the water
like man and woman
in the absence of love

Translated by Isaiah Sheffer

what remains

poetry,
a rare snake,
binds hands and learns how to perform
coiling insidiously
in the service of power

but wait, don't throw
the mantle of clouds off my shoulder
remember, in the beginning was the word,
at the end, the word distorted

eventually
there will only remain
poetry, a rare snake,
insinuating itself
into our full cup of tears

Translated by Isaiah Sheffer

the wandering Quixote

how naïve to abandon yourself
into Don Quixote's hands,
that old wielder of fish-knives
along the spine

he lifts the saucy maiden's hair
in churches and synagogues
and explains how the confusing world
and the torahs of the grand inquisitors
have gathered in the small almond on their necks

and that we will circle the earth
on the neck of the prettiest among them
while keeping time to the military parade
ah, the cynic, the pervert
humming the blues
who will set her shoes out to dry
in the display window
among showpieces
savoring how she solicits the angels
this Dulcinea with her braids cut

Translated by Andrei Codrescu

shiny soles

my darling, taking a step into risky chaos
is no harder than climbing the mountain of salt
powerlessness in this place
has the overwhelming taste of glory,
a piece of gingerbread stuffed down the throat
of those who descend into the salt mine

taking a step into risky chaos
is no worse than the woman of forty,
often seen in books,
drained by the dreary evening
on the outskirts of town,
where passion tastes like sauerkraut
and second-rate vodka
between two south American soap operas

how can I tell you, my darling,
how much longer can I tell you
that taking a step into risky chaos
is like walking on water,
with images of deaths upon deaths
reflected on shiny shoes?

Translated by Isaiah Sheffer

under the same moon

I had to come all the way here
to find that I'm a Caucasian
to see the Russian ballet,
Igor's short Ukrainian dress
in which he wrapped Paris

to bring all of it here——punishment
for those spoiled for ages
with French perfumes

I had to give all answers
and smiled at the border guard
from the other world
when I ran into the happy children
at Hanukkah
and dropped everything
in old Whitman's grass
at the spot where they may send me
to the same moon
hopefully in a different way

Translated by Andrei Codrescu

paradoxes of sleep

unlikely illusions, all white,
dreams without a trace of the shape or the soul,
of someone stretched out between the street and death

they do not sell newspapers anymore
and what they publish now are only
paradoxes, the sleep of the mind
written with impotent pens
distortions drawn with real ink

nor do they sell illusions anymore
the gates of the city have been locked

Translated by Isaiah Sheffer

submarine steps

there was a time
when we all lived our lives under the sea
in a bone city
on a white salt submarine hill

through our windows we saw
flying fish passing by
our hands could not rise up to touch the land
our eyes cold not look down at drifting clouds

through our walls we saw the water trembling
mutely moving dreams
or liquid rocking skies

and we knew nothing about time
and we knew nothing about guilt

but then our tidal walls pressed ever closer
one night our agile pearl-divers were gone
and since we had no arms nor voice
we stayed like sunken fossils on that hill

those who pass this way
can only see
a flight of ghostly stairs
beneath the sea

Translated by Isaiah Sheffer

from beyond

there is an even more distant country
than the one in which you just arrived
a homeland for every day of the week
the temptation to hide a blue steed of fire in the attic
a whinnying rover, ready to wing away with you there
where you will always arrive too late
and each time from the wrong direction
from misinterpreted desire
the way you would draw out the dream
until your worn out
flesh took the form of the wet bed-sheets
and ghost-like charged into prohibited cities
or scaled mountains long ago turned to ash
places where people tired of living in
and howling they climbed up their roofs
they twisted the birds' necks
went mad, flew, drowned
ran off wearing their entrails humming battle songs
and abandoned the country of each day of the week
where distances mean nothing anymore
where nothing is fixed any more, or eternal or stable
and no one is where you know they should be

the earth is now filled
with rovers and roaming homelands
the sky is merely a point of transit
through which the travelers savor their aimlessness

Translated by Julian Semilian

tea for one

the most difficult thing to learn
is to live alone
to put under tree bark
the body of the newborn
from which a new tree would grow

to seduce your time
like a capricious lover
who will betray you
with another woman's age
with the Father's image
descending on the face of another man
but just as unyielding

the most difficult thing is to drink your tea
in the morning together with your solitude
and to gaze at her thin fingers
stirring the sugar in your cup

Translated by Julian Semilian

wine-dark love

the sensual rhythms of the evening's voices
tap their way to the city like a blind man

your thoughts, like fish swimming in wine-dark water
with armored eyelids are blind too,
your fingers numb, your ears closed
do you not taste or smell
life's beauty
a picture smeared by its painter

love me now
we are so very much alone
our bodies vibrate within silent walls,
the price we pay for art,
we are so very much alone
and the made-up drama we play out
reveals to you what I don't know at all,
and spins out scenes that I shall never see

free spirits pass through walls and behind bars,
their breath assures us that art and quiet live.
love me now blindly, without thinking
no more newspapers, no more ashes,
shake yourself free,
we are so very much alone in wheels
of carnal rhythms

Translated by Isaiah Sheffer

life's truth

there is no such thing

the truth about the lives of others
makes good fiction
when handled by a good agent, a scam artist
confabulating destinies, retouched as you go

it's enough for the simple souls
who know nothing about St. Augustine
and are prone to believe in the axel of evil
seduced by the burgers and beer of the happy hour
while awaiting national holidays
to take advantage of sales

the truth of death is accepted by all
there are no protesters in this field
they all seem to know
what remains completely unknown

the easiest truth to sell is the image of God
whose renown, fabricated by the mass media,
rests on having survived the silence of the beginning
when the first sound broke the darkness

in His absence
the words eat each other

Translated by Julian Semilian

for the last time

I always imagined death as a woman
young and ethereal
rustling the curtains at the window

"maybe only in the Romanian language,"
my foreign lover said to me
"you have too many genders
and too much passion for catastrophes
death's a man, a silent comrade,
his shoulder against mine,
so old I've got to prop him upright"

I flew away
rustling the curtain over his shoulder
young
for the last time

Translated by Adam J. Sorkin with the poet

almost the same

after a while I began to resemble you

I saw the same patterns
in the ceiling's cracks
the same huge prehistoric beasts
in the white clouds
of a summer sky in the country,
I flicked my cigar the way you did
fingering an imagined guilt

my left eye migrated to your left eye
my hand grew at the end of your arm
we stroked the dog one after the other
and he never knew
which was me, which were you

Translated by Adam J. Sorkin with the poet

memorials

in the absence of history
the imagination fools around

every night a woman disappears
under the ruins of some empire
leaving her address a lipstick smear
on the plastic mirror,
a memorial gesture
not taken seriously here
where everything is a memorial:
days, bridges, illusions, stone parks
and the old bookkeeper
who swipes his heart through
the electronic card reader

here nobody needs heroes
the poets gather
in the Walt Whitman rest area
they compress a century
and stuff it in their pockets
politically incorrect
like harassing an eccentric dowager
with her European airs

in absence
history is just an everyday happening
floating above the ruins
a thin book tucked under one arm

Translated by Adam J. Sorkin with the poet

palms

I'm sitting with my Jewish brother
we chat about God

he's angry, I'm afraid

a line of fishermen appears
white beams on their shoulders,
pearl divers in a desert
raising the beams
to prop them against the gates

patiently he blames God
for the wanderings and the dead
whereas I cannot dream of God
except with His palms
spread wide to shelter me

I'm sitting with my Jewish brother
and we make a reckoning of the words
from the first day:
how many from light
how many from clay

Translated by Adam J. Sorkin with the poet

desire

this is no good, my unpaid guardian advise me,
don't think of poetry when it rains
loneliness is only a bad taste
memories fade when you no longer call them
just as the souls of the dead ascend
high enough not to be disturbed
by random melancholy

if a desire dawns one winter morning
snow can cover it deeply
or the horizon can fly farther away

whisper a word
and lock it back in Pandora's box
nobody will notice your tears when it rains

Translated by Adam J. Sorkin with the poet

hemispheres

yes, only you can love me
just the way you do
staring directly into my brain,
scratching your fingernail
across one hemisphere,
a secret mimosa
arrogant and vain,
and telling me I'm beautiful
though I sit at death's table,
a bouquet of neurons
preserved in a vase

never will I be so lonely
as when I'm with you
hormones float by,
stick to the walls,
objects wail in shame

but you love me the way you do
you clasp my head between your hands
and tell me
you've known me for eons
since many a sea
disappeared into the land

in secret I dream
of not crying on your shoulder
with my left brain

Translated by Adam J. Sorkin with the poet

Carmen Firan, a poet and fiction writer, has published twenty books including poetry, novels, essays and short stories in her native Romania. Since 2000 she has been living in New York. Among her recent books and publications in the United States are *Words and Flesh*, (selected works of prose, Talisman Publishers, 2008), *The Second Life* (short stories, Columbia University Press, 2005), *The Farce* (novel, Spuyten Duyvil, 2003), *In the Most Beautiful Life* (poems with photographs by Virginia Joffe, Umbrage Editions, 2002), and three collections of poetry published in New York: *Afternoon With An Angel*, *The First Moment After Death*, and *Accomplished Error*. In 2006, she edited *Born in Utopia: An Anthology of Modern and Contemporary Romanian Poetry* (Talisman House) with Paul Doru Mugur and Edward Foster, and in 2008 she co-edited the anthology *Stranger at Home. Contemporary American Poetry with an Accent* (Numina Press, Los Angeles). Firan is a member of the Pen American Center and the Poetry Society of America, and serves on the editorial boards of the international magazines *Lettre Internationale* (Paris-Bucharest) and *Interpoezia* (New York).

The translators:

Adam J. Sorkin won the Translation Prize of The Poetry Society, London, for Marin Sorescu's *The Bridge* (Bloodaxe Books, 2004), and he has been awarded NEA, Rockefeller Foundation, Academy of American Poets, Arts Council of England, Fulbright, and Witter Bynner Foundation support for his work. Sorkin is Distinguished Professor of English at Penn State Brandywine.

Julian Semilian has concentrated on translating Romanian poets of the Romanian avant-garde (Paul Celan, Tristan Tzara, Benjamin Fondane, etc). He is the Editing & Sound Department Chair at North Carolina School of the Arts.

Isaiah Sheffer is co-founder and artistic director of Symphony Space and director and host of *Selected Shorts* live and on NPR.

Andrei Codrescu, Professor of English, Louisiana State University, Commentator, National Public Radio, Editor, *Exquisite Corpse*.